To:

From:

# When Housewives Go Bad!

### By Nancy Rider Hunt

#### Introduction by Barbara Paulding

PETER PAUPER PRESS, INC.
White Plains, New York

To my dad, who always kept us laughing, and to my sister, Christy, who knows all about that. Like the time Dad unknowingly ordered and presented our mother with matching silver burial urns for their 25th wedding anniversary. When she opened the gift we all laughed until we cried, and I learned that laughter is a FABULOUS gift... especially when directed at the man in your life!

Designed by Heather Zschock

Image on cover, page 1, and page 3 adapted from photograph
© H. Armstrong Roberts/Getty Images

Illustrations copyright © 2007 Olive Sandwiches, Inc.

Copyright © 2007
Peter Pauper Press, Inc.
202 Mamaroneck Avenue
White Plains, NY 10601

ISBN 978-1-59359-888-4

Printed in China

7   6   5   4   3   2   1

Visit us at www.peterpauper.com

# When Housewives Go Bad!

# WHEN HOUSEWIVES GO BAD!

Are you ready to resign as General Manager of the Universe?

Prefer looking good to cooking good? Do you find the joys of doing laundry overrated? Wonder whatever happened to that wild woman in the mirror? Cut loose, girlfriend! Join the sisterhood of feisty females who have hung up the "Good Wife and Doting Mother" apron and gone *bad*…fabulously bad!

It's about time you claimed the whole bed for yourself once in awhile, realized that "normal" is just a setting on a washing machine, and recognized that no one should be expected to cook and clean after a long day of shopping.

You've come a long way, baby, and life is way too short to think small. Refine the charms of your inner diva as you train your loved ones to pander to your whims and passions. The game is up and the dishes may be dirty, but every good housewife knows her place—on top!

Sorry darling,
I've resigned as
general manager
of the universe.

I don't care
where he goes as
long as I don't have
to go with him!

It's okay to laugh in the bedroom so long as you don't point.

—WILL DURST

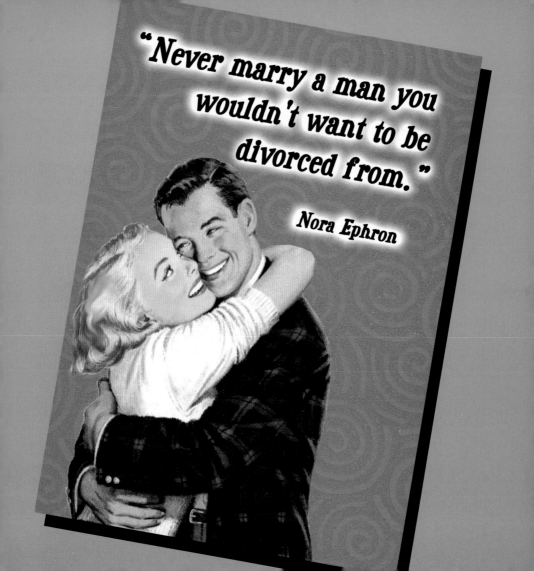

*I love the male body...*
*It's better designed*
*than the male mind!*

— ANDREA NEWMAN

With my husband
I often slip into
something more
comfortable,
like DENIAL.

My next house won't have a kitchen... just vending machines!

My husband said
he needed more
space. So I locked
him outside.

—ROSEANNE

"Normal" is nothing
more than a cycle on
a washing machine.

—WHOOPI GOLDBERG

Darling, you have a heart of gold. Let's melt it down and buy me something.

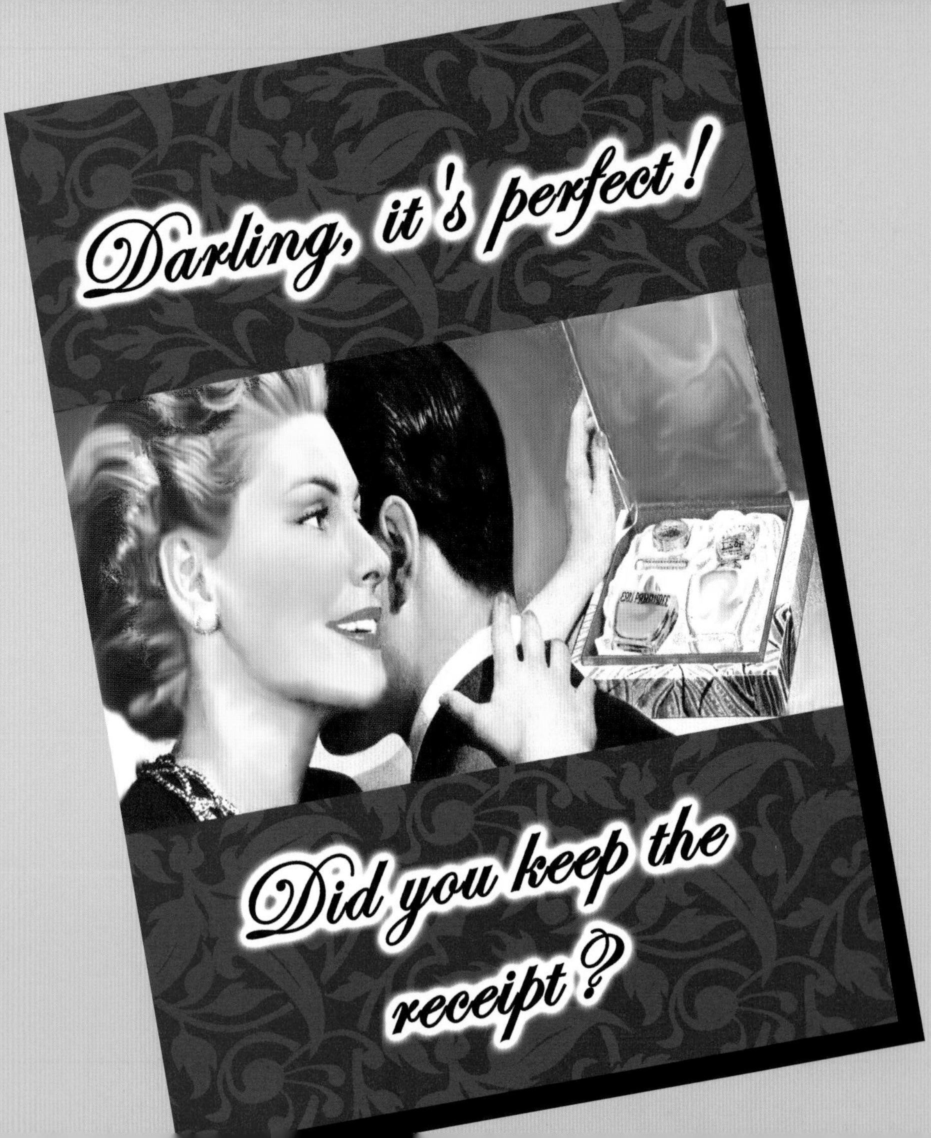
Darling, it's perfect!
Did you keep the
receipt?

She dreamed of
the single days when
she claimed the
whole bed!

She knew how to please a man but most days she chose not to.

After botox treatments,
I only LOOK like
I'm enjoying this!

My husband is an equal opportunity annoyer.

When I said "I do,"
I didn't mean laundry!

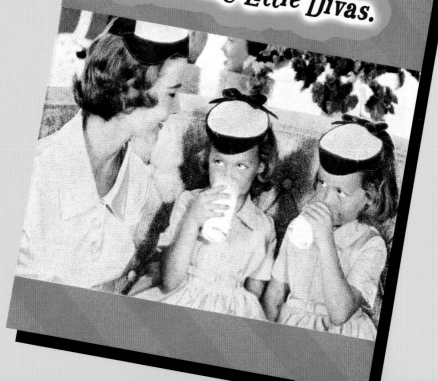

I never met a husband
I couldn't blame.

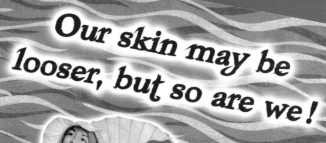

Our skin may be looser, but so are we!

"Is that your husband under your front tire, Mrs. Jones?"

The only time a woman really succeeds in changing a man is when he is a baby.

–Natalie Wood

I take my children EVERYWHERE but they keep finding their way back home!

—ROBERT ORBEN

They say marriages are made in heaven. But so is thunder and lightning!

—CLINT EASTWOOD

*If God intended for me to cook, why did He invent restaurants?*